For Jake Devine and Ethan Devine,
who know a good joke
when they hear it.

CAMP CHUCKLES

Sammy: My parents are sending me to camp.

Tammy: Why? Do you need a vacation?

Sammy: No. *They* do!

101 WACKY CAMPING JOKES

by Melvin Berger
illustrated by Don Orehek

SCHOLASTIC INC.
New York Toronto London Auckland Sydney

ISBN 0-590-45773-X

20 19 18 17   8 9/9 0 1/0

Printed in the U.S.A.   01

First Scholastic printing, June 1992

Camp Woodland is the hottest camp in the world. It's so hot that campers take turns sitting in each other's shadows!

Julie: What time is it?
Counselor: Three o'clock.
Julie: Oh, no!
Counselor: What's the matter?
Julie: I've been asking the time all day. And everybody gives me a different answer!

Every camper had a physical exam at the beginning of the summer.

"What's the most you've ever weighed?" the doctor asked Tim.

"Ninety-two pounds," Tim told the doctor.

"And what's the least you've ever weighed?" the doctor asked.

"Eight pounds, four ounces," Tim answered.

Mitch came into his cabin with holes
cut all over his shirt.

"What happened?" asked Nancy.

"We were playing cat and mouse. And
I was the Swiss cheese!"

Judy: Is grape jelly very expensive?

Trudy: No.

Judy: Then why did the counselor yell at me when I spilled a whole jar on Bob's new shirt?

Dan: I'm as tall as you are.

Stan: No, you're not. I'm a head taller than you.

Dan: Well, I'm as tall as you at the other end. My feet go down as far as yours!

Does horseback riding give you a headache?

No. The very opposite!

It's very damp at Camp Arrowhead. When they set a mousetrap, they catch a fish!

One day, Steve's baseball cap was missing. He said that Ron had taken it.

The counselor asked Ron, "Did you take Steve's cap?"

"Absolutely, positively not!" insisted Ron.

"OK, I believe you," said the counselor.

"In that case," said Ron, "can I keep the cap?"

New Camper: I thought you said this camp has no mosquitoes.

Old Camper: That's right. These mosquitoes come from the camp down the road!

One day the counselor got a phone call. It was from a camper who had been at camp the summer before. The old camper said, "I thought of camp yesterday."

"Why?" the counselor asked. "Where were you?"

"At the garbage dump!" the old camper answered.

Jerry: I beat my friends up every
  morning.
Adam: Really?
Jerry: Yes. I'm up at seven o'clock.
  They all sleep until eight!

Tina: I just touched some poison ivy.
Nina: That was a rash thing to do.

Jimmy: I was so mad I could have punched Arthur in the nose!
Pete: Well, what stopped you?
Jimmy: Arthur!

The campers went for a hike on a very hot day. Claudia talked without stopping during the trip. When they got back she found that her tongue was sunburned!

Tom: I just found a horseshoe.

Ellie: That's good luck.

Tom: No, it's not. It just means some poor horse is running around barefooted!

How did you find the weather at camp?

It was easy. I just went outside — and there it was!

Penny's mother sent her some new sneakers. When they arrived at camp, Penny tried to put them on. "Ouch!" she cried. "These sneakers hurt!"

Cathy was watching from the next bunk. "Of course they hurt. You put them on the wrong feet!"

Penny thought for a moment. "But these are the only feet I have," she answered.

Marty came into his cabin with his clothes all torn. Norman asked him, "Did you have an accident?"

"No," said Marty. "A bull threw me over a fence."

"But that's an accident," said Norman.

"No, it's not. The bull did it on purpose!" Marty insisted.

Mother: Did you win a prize for horseback riding?

Son: No, I didn't. Only *horrible* mention.

At the end of camp, Julie won the prize for neatest trunk. Her mother was amazed.

"How did your trunk get so neat?" she asked her messy daughter.

"It was easy," said Julie. "I just never unpacked!"

Did you hear about the mosquito that bit everybody in the camp cabin?

He passed the screen test!

On the last day of camp everyone was asked the same question: "What is the best part of camp?"

One wise guy answered, "Going home!"

COUNTRY CAPERS

Camper: Is it easy to milk a cow?
Farmer: Sure it is. Any jerk can do it.

Farmer: My son left the farm. Now he polishes shoes in the city.
Camper: Oh, you make hay while the *son* shines!

A hunter with a rifle wandered into the campgrounds.

"Where are you going with that rifle?" Carol asked.

"I'm looking for bears," answered the hunter.

"There are no bears," said Carol.

"That's why I'm looking for them," answered the hunter.

While visiting a farm, some campers saw a farmer with a big load of manure.

"What are you going to do with the manure?" one of the campers asked.

"I'm going to spread it on the strawberries," replied the farmer.

"That's funny," said the camper. "At camp we spread sugar and cream on our strawberries!"

Farmer: What would you do if a bull charged you?

Mary: I'd pay whatever it charged!

Why did the owl go, "Tweet, tweet"?

Because he didn't give a hoot!

Little Seymour saw his first snake. "Come quickly," he called out. "I just found a tail without a dog!"

Camp Woodland was across the road from a dairy farm. One day the kids saw a large bull.

"Is that bull safe?" someone asked the farmer.

"Safer than you are!" was his answer.

Farmer: Cows are not good dancers.
Camper: How do you know?
Farmer: They have two left feet!

Camper: Look at that bunch of cows.
Farmer: Not bunch, herd.
Camper: Heard what?
Farmer: Of cows.
Camper: Sure I've heard of cows.
Farmer: No, I mean a cowherd.
Camper: So what? I have no secrets
from cows!

Camper: What are you growing here?
Farmer: Potatoes and onions.
Camper: How's the crop?
Farmer: Not too good. All I get is
potatoes with eyes wet from crying!

Joe: This is a good place for a picnic.

Jane: How do you know?

Joe: All these flies and ants must know what they're doing!

Why do cows wear bells around their necks?

Because their horns don't work.

LETTER LAFFS

Steve wrote home. "I'm glad you named me Steve," he said in the letter.

"Why?" his mother asked in her reply.

"Because that's what all the kids at camp call me," he wrote back.

Kathy wanted to mail her first letter home from camp. She went to the post office to buy a stamp.

"Do I stick the stamp on myself?" she asks the clerk.

"No. Stick it on the envelope!"

What are the two shortest camp letters ever written?

Dear Dad,
No fun.
Your son

Dear Son,
Too bad.
Your dad

Josh sent a letter to his folks. He told about a ten-mile hike he had taken.

His father wrote back saying, "In my day I thought nothing of walking ten miles."

Josh wrote back, "To tell the truth, I didn't think much of it either."

Mom and Dad got this letter from Junior: "I had fun today diving into the pool. But they say I'll have even more fun when they put in the water!"

Martin ended a letter to his dad with this question, "Is Washington's picture still on the dollar bill?"

His father wrote back, "Of course it is. Why do you ask?"

Martin answered, "Because it's been so long since I've seen one!"

I got a letter from my sister. She just had a baby. But she didn't say whether it's a boy or girl. So I don't know if I'm an uncle or an aunt!

CAMPING MADNESS

Mike and Pat went hunting. Mike saw a large goose fly by. He raised his rifle to shoot.

"Don't waste your time," Pat hollered. "The rifle is not loaded."

"I can't wait," Mike shouted back. "The bird will be gone if I take the time to load!"

A city boy was on his first camping trip. He was eating his lunch under a tree when an old-timer came along.

"It smells like rain," he said to the boy.

The city boy replied, "They said it was lemonade."

Have you ever hunted bear?

No. But I once went fishing in shorts!

John was hard at work with the broom in his family's tent.

His mother came in and said, "That's nice. Are you sweeping out the tent?"

"No," John answered. "I'm sweeping out the dirt."

Cindy and Mindy were walking through a field. Suddenly they saw a huge bull heading toward them. Cindy started shaking.

"Don't act so scared," her friend said.

"I'm not acting!" Cindy muttered.

Terry and Debbie were camping with their parents deep in the woods.

"How far is it to town?" Terry wanted to know.

"Six miles," said Debbie.

"That's too far to walk," Terry replied.

"It's not too bad," Debbie said. "We can each walk three miles!"

George went fishing, but at the end of the day he had not caught one fish.

On the way back to camp, he stopped at a fish store.

"I want to buy three trout," he said to the owner. "But instead of putting them in a bag, throw them to me."

"Why should I do that?" the owner asked.

"So I can tell everyone that I caught three fish!"

A man walked into a lodge in Yellowstone National Park. "Can you give me a room and bath?" he asked the clerk.

"I can give you a room," the clerk said. "But you'll have to take the bath by yourself!"

Dick and Bob were on a hunting trip. At nightfall, Dick complained, "We've been hunting all day. We've shot at five deer — and not hit one!"

"OK. Let's miss two more and then head back to camp," said Bob.

Bob: Did you hear about the camper who was killed by a garter snake?

Betty: That's impossible. A garter snake is not poisonous.

Bob: It doesn't have to be if it can make you jump off a cliff!

Scott was hiking in Utah when a bear suddenly appeared. The grizzly rushed at Scott. But it jumped too far and went over Scott's head.

Scott started running the other way. Again the bear caught up and jumped over Scott's head.

Finally Scott saw a tree and he climbed it.

When he looked down he saw the bear practicing short jumps!

The Rocky Mountains are very big and far apart. It takes a long time for an echo to bounce back off one of these mountains.

One night, a camper in the Rockies went to sleep early. But before climbing into his sleeping bag he yelled, "Time to get up."

And eight hours later the echo came back and woke him up!

Dawn was breaking over the camp-grounds. Tony and Steve were lying in their tent.

"That was a terrible thunder and lightning storm last night," Tony announced.

Steve turned to him and said, "Why didn't you wake me up? You know I can't sleep during a storm!"

COUNSELORS' CRACK-UPS

The head counselor gathered all the campers together. To get their attention, the counselor called out, "Order! Order!"

In a flash someone shouted out, "Hamburger, Coke, and French fries!"

The counselor was greeting the new campers.

"So you decided to come to camp," she said to one.

"Nope," the camper answered. "I was *sent* to camp!"

Sonny: I can't sleep. What should I do?
Counselor: Lie near the edge of the bed. That way you'll be sure to drop off!

One evening, a counselor saw Max on his hands and knees. "What are you doing?" she asked.

"I'm looking for my dollar bill," Max replied. "I lost it down the road."

"Why don't you look for it there?"

"Because the light's better here!"

The next day the counselor saw Stan pulling at his pockets.

"What happened?" she asked.

"I lost my dollar bill," Stan said. "And I've looked in every pocket except one."

"Why don't you look there?"

"Because if it's not there I'll kill myself!"

"I can't find my dollar bill," Jane sobbed.

"Don't worry," her counselor said. "A dollar doesn't go very far today."

Lunch was just over. Brian was about to jump into the lake.

"It's dangerous to swim on a full stomach," warned his counselor."

"Don't worry," Brian said. "I'll do the backstroke."

Counselor: How many times did I tell you to make your bed?

Jane: I can't answer. I didn't know I was supposed to keep count!

Wanda: A fish just bit my toe.
Counselor: Which one?
Wanda: I don't know. All the fish look
  alike to me!

The counselor was talking to the campers about safety. She said, "Don't climb any trees. If you fall down and break a leg, don't come running to me!"

Counselor: A camper just swallowed a bullet. What should I do?

Camp Doctor: Don't point him at anyone.

Counselor: A camper just swallowed a roll of film. What should I do?

Camp Doctor: Don't worry. Nothing will develop.

Counselor: A camper just swallowed a pen. What should I do?

Camp Doctor: Use a pencil.

Counselor: Why did I catch you grabbing an extra cookie?

Laura: Because I didn't hear you coming.

Counselor: This is a dogwood tree.

Ben: How do you know?

Counselor: By its bark.

Counselor: Why are you sitting up in bed?

Ruth: There's a mosquito in the cabin.

Counselor: But it hasn't bitten you.

Ruth: I know. But it came so close I could hear its motor.

Counselor: Swimming keeps you fit and trim.

Don: I guess you never saw a whale!

Counselor: Eat your spinach. It's good for growing kids.

Monica: Who wants to grow kids?

Sarah: I dropped my watch in the river. But it's still running.

Counselor: Really?

Sarah: Oh, yes. The river keeps running!

Lee: I just swallowed a fish bone!

Counselor: Are you choking?

Lee: No, I'm serious!

Counselor: Wash your face. I can see what you had for breakfast.

Henry: If you're so smart, what did I have?

Counselor: Eggs.

Henry: Wrong. I had eggs yesterday!

Counselor: Jake, why did you put that snake in Annie's bed?

Jake: Because I couldn't find a frog!

A counselor saw a camper sitting alone. "Why don't you play with your friends?" he asked.

"Because I have only one friend," the girl replied. "And I hate her!"

Counselor: Who gave you that black eye?

Camper: No one gave it to me. I had to fight for it!

My counselor doesn't know anything about kids. She makes me go to sleep when I'm wide awake. And then she wakes me up when I'm fast asleep!

Camper: There's a leak over my bunk!
Counselor: Don't complain. It only
leaks when it rains.

Camper: There's a leak over my bunk!
Counselor: Shh! Don't make such a
fuss. Soon everyone will want one!

Camper: There's a leak over my bunk!

Counselor: That's what we said in the camp ads: Running water in every cabin!

DAFFY DOINGS

Ben looked at the ham slice in his sandwich. It was very, very thin.

"Did you cut this ham?" Ben asked the camp cook.

"Yes," the cook replied.

"Well, you almost missed!" said Ben.

Ellen: I'd like to be in the camp show.

Show Director: Have you ever acted before?

Ellen: Well, my arm was once in a cast.

Jo: I've broken my glasses. Do I have to be examined all over again?

Camp Doctor: No. Just your eyes!

Brad: Here's my drawing of a horse and wagon.

Arts and Crafts Counselor: I see the horse. But where's the wagon?

Brad: The horse will draw the wagon.

Camper: I'm having trouble with my breathing.

Camp Doctor: I'll give you something to stop that.

Meg's mother was visiting her daughter at camp. "How did you find the steak at dinner?" she asked.

"With a magnifying glass!"

Jane's mother asked her daughter, "How did you find the steak?

"I just moved the potatoes, and there it was!" Jane replied.

Bonnie: Is this a ham sandwich?

Cook: What does it taste like?

Bonnie: I can't tell.

Cook: Then what difference does it make?

John: What did you think of Suzy's dancing in the talent show?

Jane: Suzy would be a great dancer except for two things — her feet!

Camper: There's something wrong with my hot dog.

Cook: Don't tell me. I'm not a veterinarian.

Sara fell and broke her arm. The camp doctor put it in a sling.

"Will I be able to play the piano when my arm heals?" Sara asked the doctor.

"Sure you will," the doctor replied.

"That's amazing!" said Sara. "I never took a lesson in my life!"

Jack went to see the camp nurse. "I fell last night," he said. "And I was unconscious for eight hours."

The nurse was shocked. "How awful. What happened?"

"I fell asleep!"

Patty went to the arts and crafts shack. The counselor asked, "Would you like to make some paper dolls?"

"No, thanks," said Patty. "I cut that out long ago."

Pierre was a camper from France. In his honor, Jenny sang a French song in the talent show. But she didn't sing very well.

"Does that make you homesick?" someone asked Pierre.

"No," he answered. "Just sick sick!"

Camp Doctor: Your cough sounds better today.

Camper: It should. I practiced all night!

Camp Woodland put on a show with a happy ending. Everybody was glad when it was over.